ENNEAGRAM
every day

ENNEAGRAM
every day

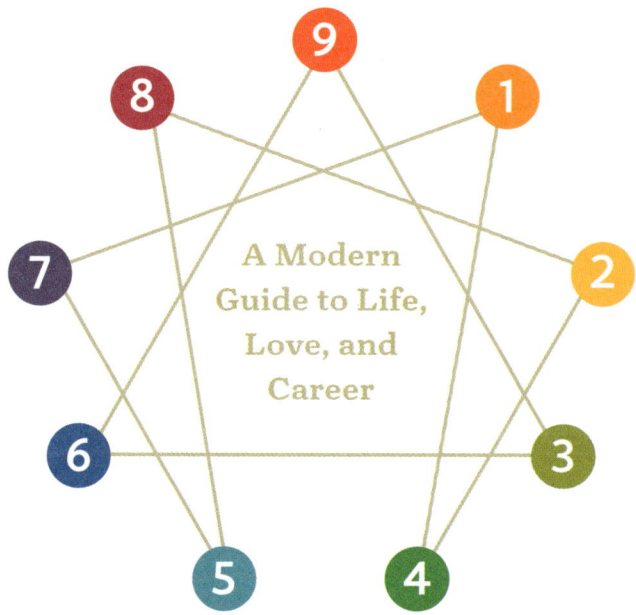

A Modern
Guide to Life,
Love, and
Career

DAYO AJANAKU

illustrated by **ELEANOR GROSCH**

RUNNING PRESS
PHILADELPHIA

Running Press
Hachette Book Group
1290 Avenue of the Americas, New York, NY 10104
www.runningpress.com
@Running_Press

First Edition: July 2025

Published by Running Press, an imprint of Hachette Book Group, Inc. The Running Press name and logo are trademarks of Hachette Book Group, Inc.

The Hachette Speakers Bureau provides a wide range of authors for speaking events. To find out more, go to www.hachettespeakersbureau.com or email HachetteSpeakers@hbgusa.com.

Running Press books may be purchased in bulk for business, educational, or promotional use. For more information, please contact your local bookseller or the Hachette Book Group Special Markets Department at Special.Markets@hbgusa.com.

The publisher is not responsible for websites (or their content) that are not owned by the publisher.

Print book cover and interior design by Susan Van Horn

Library of Congress Control Number: 2024949575

ISBNs: 978-0-7624-8978-7 (hardcover), 979-8-89414-097-1 (ebook)

Printed in China

APS

10 9 8 7 6 5 4 3 2 1

*This book is dedicated to every teacher,
coach, supporter, and friend who has
walked with me on this Enneagram journey.
This book could not have been created
without the love, support, and wisdom you
all have poured into me. Forever grateful.*

Contents

Chapter Three:

The Nine Types in Career

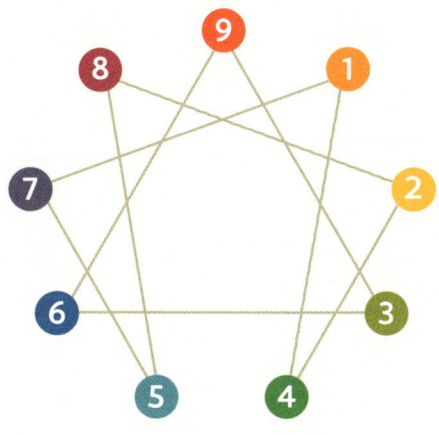

Introduction

IF THIS IS YOUR FIRST BOOK ON THE ENNEAGRAM OF Personality, you've likely heard of this personality typing system through a friend, a family member, or even on the internet or social media. The Enneagram of Personality has had a significant impact on the personality and spiritual world in the United States since its beginnings. Many have engaged with the Enneagram to gain wisdom, social insight, and even spiritual growth.

The Enneagram of Personality, known more simply as the Enneagram, is an ancient personality typing system that draws on modern psychology and spiritual principles. The origins of the Enneagram have philosophical roots in ancient Greece with diverse roots in spirituality. Contemporary influences from psychiatrists and philosophers throughout the twentieth century have molded this personality typing system into the popular test we know (and love) today. Two well-known people—Oscar Ichazo, a South American philosopher, and Claudio Naranjo, a Chilean psychiatrist—had huge influences on the Enneagram; we still use their Enneagram model today.

The word *Enneagram* is derived from the Greek words *ἐννέα*, meaning "nine," and *γράμμα* meaning "written" or "drawn." This unique system places people's personalities into one of nine distinct personality types through different techniques. Whichever numerical category you fall into serves as your main type. When illustrated, the Enneagram numbers (or types) are organized in a clocklike circle, where numbers one through nine are ordered next to each other—with number one in the same position as it is on an analog clock—and arrows connect the numbers within the circle.

As you will come to learn, each of the nine Enneagram types has different desires, motivations, and fears. Two individuals can exhibit similar behaviors, but their motivations may differ greatly from one person to the next. When used correctly, the Enneagram has the power to influence the quality of your everyday life. It can speak truth to the areas of your life that are hidden behind fear and anxiety, and it can set you free from negative patterns that can affect the ways in which you show up in the world and in your own life. The Enneagram calls you back to your essence while teaching you to appreciate the ways your personality protects you from emotional and mental—and even physical—harm. It can enlighten you, revealing that your personality is a tool for personal success, growth, and abundance.

Tips For Identifying Your Main Type

Perhaps the hardest part about using the Enneagram is finding your main type. Different factors contribute to how your main type is formed. Our main type is set at birth and cultivated through interactions with family, friends, and the world at large. Oftentimes, people who take the test early in life find that their type changes as they grow older and figure out who they are outside of the opinion and thoughts of others. But this is not true for everyone.

Finding your main type is an art more than it is a science. The most popular way to find your type is to take a test administered by a credible source. The issue with this method is that we are not always self-aware and can be unsure of what is true for us. We often choose the answer that we wish we were and not the answer that we actually are. Taking the test as a consciously unaware person (which we all are at some point in our lives) may lead to inaccurate results, but it can work for those who are open to seeing the truth about who they are and unafraid of what they see on the other side.

Another way people choose to find their type is by reading books like this! Reading the descriptions of all nine types is a helpful way to find your type, since type descriptions tend to be neutral in books. Rather than proposing questions, they state the facts of each type, and you can determine what resonates with you. Typically, what you should be looking for are the type's core desires, motivations, and fears. The characteristic descriptions may (or may not) resonate due to differences in social, economic, and/or gender positioning in the world, but most things should ring true.

Another way to discover your type is by participating in typing interviews with an Enneagram coach. Depending on the experience and cultural competency of the coach, this can be a helpful tool. Inaccuracies may arise, however, since a coach can lack understanding of the interviewee's social position, and the coach may not consciously take these things into account. No matter how well-crafted the questions the interviewer asks, you can fall into the same predicament that you'd find yourself in by taking a self-administered test: an inability to be self-aware enough to know what your honest answer is. Having another person ask you questions can also lead to mistyping because we all want to be perceived well by people, even if they are strangers. Because of this self-serving bias, we are unlikely to tell the whole truth about ourselves if we feel that it may leave a poor impression on the person we are engaging with. However, a good Enneagram coach can see past the projections and get to the heart of what your motivations are if they know what to listen for. When choosing an Enneagram coach, ask about their teachers, where they learned about the Enneagram, and how the Enneagram has impacted them. Reputable companies like the Narrative Tradition, the International Enneagram Association, and Trinity Transition Consultants are all recommended places to find credible Enneagram coaches.

My advice is to explore all three of these avenues within a group of trusted Enneagram communities or with open-minded and curious friends and family. An Enneagram test that I recommend can be found on Dr. Deborah Egerton's website (www.deborahegerton.com). Dr. Egerton is an Enneagram + Inclusion, Diversity, Equity & Anti-racism specialist, so the test she provides recognizes and considers differences in culture and upbringing.

Allow each thing to confirm another and bring in people whom you know, love, and trust to speak to your type. It is normal to get different results from these methods.

Continue learning about the types. Accept where you are and allow your type to reveal itself to you when the time is right.

One aspect of the Enneagram that differentiates it from all other personality typing systems is that we each have all nine types within us. We lean on and take traits from types that are not our main type and will likely resonate with certain type traits outside of our own. This is normal and in alignment with the natural belief that we are all one—more alike than we are different. We all want to be good, loved, valued, special, competent, safe, satisfied, protected, and at peace. If you feel that all nine types resonate with you, take a closer look at the Type Nine personality and traits. Oftentimes, Type Nines will find themselves able to relate to almost every type because of their agreeable and harmonic personalities.

As someone who has read numerous books on the Enneagram; spoken to dozens of people about their type; listened to podcasts; attended trainings, seminars, and conferences on the Enneagram, I still incorrectly guess people's types. It is important that we honor everyone's own understanding and expression of their type, even if it is contrary to what we think we know.

Unique Elements of the Enneagram

While everyone has one main type, the expression of their type can be heavily influenced by numerous factors, like which wing they lean on (wings are the numbers next to yours), their growth/stress arrows, and their overall cultural, political, and social standing in the world. Individuals with the same type will likely connect on a deep level, but the expressions of their types will differ, depending on these factors. Your cultural, social, and political standing will heavily influence the way your Enneagram type shows up as well. Two Type Threes who come from contrasting societal positions can express their Type Three-ness much differently, to the point where it may be difficult to recognize that they are both the same main type.

Let's circle back to the Enneagram type wings. Wings are the numbers next to your main type number on the Enneagram symbol. Each of the nine main types has two options for wings: Type One has Nine or Two; Type Two has Three or One; Type Three has Two or Four; Type Four has Three or Five; Type Five has Four or Six; Type Six has Five or Seven; Type Seven has Six or Eight. Type Eight has Seven or Nine; Type Nine has Eight or One. When written, wings are represented with a lowercase w. You may see someone write "1w2" or "2w3." These translate to "Enneagram

Type One with a wing number Two" and "Enneagram Type Two with a wing number Three," respectively.

Wings are the facets of your personality that you use when you're in different social settings. You may lean on one wing when you're with your family but use the other wing when you're out with friends, at work, on a date, or in any other environment. This is your way of attempting to fit in and meet situations in a way that yields the most favorable outcome for everyone. Drawing on the influence of your wings is a fundamental tool in your Enneagram tool belt. Wings aren't always in use, though. You have the option of engaging one wing over the other, or you can use both wings simultaneously—and even use neither. Wings answer this question: "Who do I need to be in order to thrive in this environment?"

Another important part of the Enneagram that influences type expression are growth and stress arrows. Growth arrows are sometimes called "the path of integration" and stress arrows "the path of disintegration." This pair of numbers has also been called "the path of health and unhealthy." My favorite way of referring to these arrows was coined by Chichi Agorom, a certified Enneagram teacher and practitioner, and author of *The Enneagram for Black Liberation*, who calls them "movements towards consciousness and movements towards unconsciousness." No matter what you call them, each type flows to the designated numbers that the arrows are connected to in both growth and stress. You can find out what number you go to in growth or stress by looking at the arrows connected to your main type number in the image on page xviii. If the arrow is pointing away from your main type number, you're going toward stress/disintegration/unhealth/unconsciousness. If the arrow is pointing toward your main type number, then that is the number you go to in growth/integration/health/consciousness.

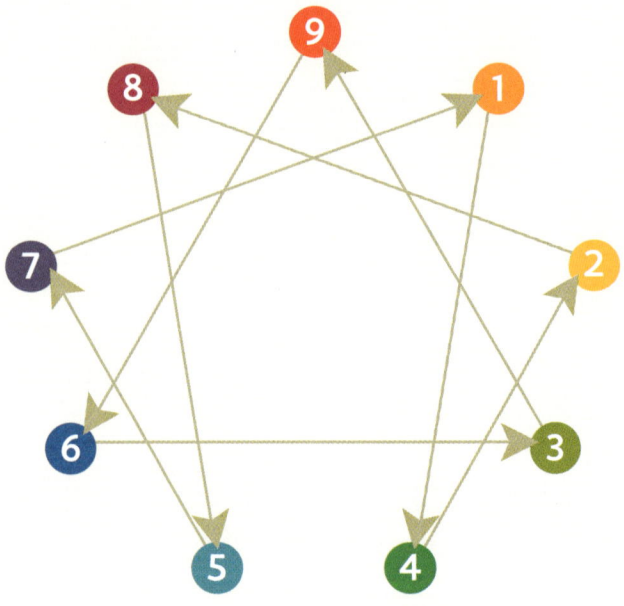

In practice, everyone will experience the growth and stress arrows differently. Many people experience the low side of both their growth and stress numbers when they are stressed and the high side of both numbers when they are experiencing growth. As an example, the main Type One goes to Type Seven in growth and Type Four in stress. When Type One is stressed, they can experience the low side of both the Seven and the Four. You may see a stressed Type One begin to find ways to avoid pain by staying busy like a Type Seven or become overly moody and sensitive like a Type Four. But when Type Ones are in growth, they can experience the high side of both the Seven and the Four. Type Ones in growth find it easier to be spontaneous and joyful, like the Type Seven, and turn their pain into creativity like the Type Four. Knowing which numbers you go to in growth and stress can help you become more aware of your emotional standing. As you digest this information, be sure to consider not only your main type but also your wings and growth and stress types.

The objective of this book is to explore the ways you can use the Enneagram in your everyday life—to foster growth and improvement both within yourself and within your relationships. The Enneagram should be used not to become a stereotypical version of your main type but to get back to the essence of who you truly are. It is a tool you can pick up and put down depending on whatever situation, environment, and headspace you may find yourself in. But do remember: We are our essence, not our type.

CHAPTER ONE

The Nine Types Moving Through Life

EACH ENNEAGRAM TYPE HAS UNIQUE GIFTS TO offer and challenges they face, which work together to create type structure. There is no type that is better than another. They each have work to do to get back to the essence of who they are outside of their type structure and personality. Personality is a combination of nature and nurture. We are born with our types, but our types are nurtured into solid form as we move through the world and encounter situations and circumstances that confirm it. Some people grow up in environments that allow their type to flourish because the characteristics they exhibit are beneficial to the society they live in. Others' types are stifled because their environments do not affirm their core desires and fears. For example, in an individualist culture, where people are encouraged to look out for themselves and create their own identity separate from the collective, the independent and creative Type Four's structure may thrive. However, in a collectivist culture, where people are encouraged to constantly act as a helping hand and look out for their neighbor, the compassionate and caring Type Two structure may thrive. Keep in mind that many behavioral characteristics can be shared across types, so to figure out your own type, pay attention to which desires and fears speak to you the most.

Furthermore, I will give a breakdown of some of the behaviors each type may exhibit as they navigate their life. I will also give examples of each type found in media, so that you have real-world examples of them experiencing and dealing with relatable situations.

TYPE

1

THE FIRST TYPE OF THE ENNEAGRAM IS SOMETIMES called the Perfectionist or the Reformer. A Type One's core desire is to be seen as a good person by themselves and by others. Their core motivation is fueled by a desire to see both themselves and the world restored to perfect order and to see all wrongs made right. They tend to be full of integrity, focusing their energy on improving the world around them, as well as improving themselves. Type Ones are the people we go to when we need astute attention to detail. They have a great eye for seeing where things are falling short, and they usually know exactly how to fix it. Ones are known for their incredibly high standards. Not only do they hold themselves to these high standards, but they have a tendency to hold others to them as well.

The Type One values integrity, honesty, and truth above all. They may struggle with self-righteousness and hypercriticism of themselves and others because they can see the flaws of the world so clearly. The One's core fear is being seen as bad or corrupt. A factor that can help you determine if you are a Type One is whether you possess an aggressive inner critic who attempts to dictate your every move. Type Ones must battle this internal voice that reminds them of right and wrong and who sees the world in a very black-and-white way. As the name suggests, many Ones struggle with some form of perfectionism, but the manner in which that manifests differs depending on the individual.

An example of a Type One in media is Whitley Gilbert from the TV show *A Different World*. Throughout the show, Whitley struggles with perfectionism that manifests in her being incredibly rigid and unkind to those who do not meet her personal standards. As Whitley's character develops, she begins to recognize the ways in which her rigidity is getting in the way of her relationships, thus causing her to reflect and become much warmer and more agreeable.

TYPE

2

THE ENNEAGRAM TYPE TWO IS SOMETIMES CALLED the Helper or the Giver. A Type Two's core desire is to be seen as a loving person by themselves and by others. Their core motivation is fueled by a desire to be useful and irreplaceable in the eyes of those they love and respect. Type Twos have a strong need to be needed. They often struggle with setting boundaries because they see themselves as needing to always be available for the greater good. Type Twos are highly relational people. They are incredible cheerleaders who support their friends, family, and coworkers in whatever endeavors they undertake.

A Type Two's core fear is being unloved. When presented with a need, they may struggle to say no out of fear that they will be seen as disposable. They often struggle with knowing what they need and instead find themselves preoccupied with the needs and wants of others.

If they are not careful, Type Twos can easily neglect themselves in their pursuit of helpfulness. Acceptance is vital to the Enneagram Type Two. It is incredibly important to them that the people around them feel unconditionally loved. Twos will shape-shift and adapt to provide this for the people in their environment, often to their detriment. Type Twos are incredibly gentle, soft, and kind people. They are the best people to go to for sound advice because they are great listeners. People often consider Type Twos experts at knowing other people's needs before those people may recognize that they need it. This can sometimes feel smothering for the individuals on the receiving end, especially if the help is not sought.

An example of a Type Two in media is Synclaire James-Jones from the TV Show *Living Single*. Synclaire would often find herself serving the goals and needs of others instead of focusing on her own. It wasn't until she found her own passions and purpose that she began to enforce better boundaries for herself and honor her own needs. Though difficult, Synclaire went from being the assistant of her cousin Khadijah James to pursuing her own passion for being an actress.

TYPE

3

THE ENNEAGRAM TYPE THREE IS SOMETIMES CALLED the Achiever or the Performer. A Type Three's core desire is to be seen as a valuable person by themselves and by others. Their core motivation is fueled by a desire to create a life that is worthwhile both to themselves and others. They are driven to succeed in the way that their social environment defines success, which is unique to their community. Not all Threes seek flashy clothes, cars, and other pricey material possessions, especially if those things are not considered status symbols in their community. Threes want to be affirmed and admired for what they have achieved. They want to be the best at what they do and can be hyperaware of how others perceive them. To them, image is everything. Threes are highly efficient individuals. They know the quickest way to do things and are always looking for ways to make their lives more efficient, whether that be a new app or a new method of completing a task.

Threes are charismatic people who lead with enthusiasm and high energy. They make incredible entrepreneurs because of how adaptable and driven they are. A Three's productivity can be a strength in moments where there is a lot to get done, but this can lead to burnout. Threes often don't recognize their limits and attempt to do whatever they can to get positive feedback from their peers. Type Threes know exactly what is expected of them and they know exactly what needs to be done to get the validation and praise they crave.

A Type Three's core fear is being seen as worthless. Threes often struggle to answer the question, *Who am I outside of what I do?* Once they reach retirement, Threes may find it difficult to rest and enjoy the life they have built because of how they have attached themselves and their identity to their work. Threes may also struggle with competitiveness. They may find that they create competition where it is not needed due to their burning desire to be the best at whatever they do.

An example of a Type Three in media is the character Molly Carter from the TV show *Insecure*. Molly is an attorney who, after moving from her predominantly white law firm to a predominantly Black law firm, finds herself at odds with her new coworkers because her previous law firm did things more efficiently than her new firm does. Molly eventually learns that obsessing over efficiency can get in the way of building invaluable relationships.

TYPE

THE ENNEAGRAM TYPE FOUR IS SOMETIMES CALLED the Individualist or the Creative. A Type Four's core desire is to be seen as a special or unique person by themselves and others. Their core motivation is the pursuit of difference, which can be expressed through many means but typically through creative outlets. Type Fours want to feel deeply known and understood by others. A defining characteristic of a Four is their ability to tap into deep emotions, thoughts, and feelings. The high side of this is that they can be incredibly empathetic, compassionate, and understanding. The low side is that they can become emotional and hyperfocused on their own inner world. They often isolate themselves and become moody when they feel that life is difficult. Type Fours are gifted at expressing the human experience in innovative ways. They prefer to relate to others who also seek relational depth. Fours typically express their individuality through fashion and personal style, but not all of them do this.

The Type Four's core fear is that they are missing something or are incomplete. An emotion that Fours often over-identify with is melancholy and sadness. They embrace dark emotions more than others do, and they savor the complexities that come with these emotions. Authenticity is of high value for Type Fours. They avoid fads and trends and would rather miss out on things simply because too many other people are involved. They long to show up in their lives as true to themselves as possible. They do not want to be carbon copies of anyone and desire to express their individuality. Many artists and actors are Type Fours. They care deeply about their craft and want to inspire others to do good, creative work as well. Type Fours may have many admirers throughout their life, not only for their authenticity but also for their vision. It is of utmost importance for Fours to be in alignment with their core values in every area of their life, including work, religion, friendships, romantic relationships, etc. A life that feels disingenuous to a Type Four is a life they cannot comfortably live in.

An example of a Type Four in media is the character Moesha from the TV show *Moesha*. Throughout the show, Moesha finds solace in journaling her thoughts, and she expresses herself through her unique fashion sense and poetry. Moesha struggles with creating drama and unnecessary chaos in her life just so she can feel *something*. Many of her relationships—especially the one with her step-mother, Dee—are strained because of Moesha's inability to access emotions that do not serve her melancholy.

TYPE

5

THE ENNEAGRAM TYPE FIVE IS SOMETIMES REFERRED to as the Investigator or the Observer. A Type Five's core desire is to be seen as a competent person by themselves and others. Their core motivation is acquiring knowledge and mastery. Fives work hard to accumulate all the information and knowledge they can to help themselves feel well-equipped to manage the world around them. Like Type Fours (the Individualists), Type Fives can be the withdrawn type that retreat into their inner worlds, without participating out of fear that they will drain the limited energy they possess. Type Fives are often known as the kind of people who live a minimalist lifestyle and can survive on very little. They know what is essential and let go of the rest.

Another defining characteristic for Fives is their innate ability to be objective. Their objectivity has both low and high sides. On the low side, this objectivity can look like mental compartmentalization, where feelings and emotions are unnecessary. Many people perceive Fives as cold because of this tendency to compartmentalize. On the high side, this objectivity reflects the ability to remain neutral, providing unbiased feedback and advice. Fives are very protective of their time, space, and energy. They recognize that they have a finite amount of time, space, and energy, so they prefer to be selective with whom and how they spend their resources. Fives are excellent at establishing boundaries, but sometimes their boundaries can be overly rigid. This rigidity may make them lose out on certain friendships and relationships because others may see them as overly independent. They can be perceived as difficult to open up to, which can make it hard to get to know them. Fives are considered the experts of the Enneagram. They find great fulfillment in taking deep dives and researching topics that interest them just for the sake of knowledge. Fives may also struggle with acknowledging and meeting their own physical and relational needs. They often deny themselves for the sake of self-preservation.

Type Fives are uncommon within media, but the character Shuri from the movie *Black Panther: Wakanda Forever* is a great example of one. When facing the problem of how to save Wakanda from the Talokan army after the loss of her father, brother, and mother, Shuri turns to knowledge and science to revive the Black Panther and defeat her enemies. She compartmentalizes, pushing her grief to the side to focus on and successfully achieve her mission. However, Shuri does all of this with the help of a fellow trusted scientist who supports her and constantly urges her to take care of herself—something Type Fives must learn to accept and eventually do on their own.

TYPE

6

THE ENNEAGRAM TYPE SIX IS SOMETIMES CALLED THE Loyalist or the Loyal Skeptic. A Type Six's core desire is to be seen as a committed person by themselves and others. They are motivated by a desire to ensure that they have guidance and direction in their lives. Because of this, many Sixes develop amazing teamwork skills; they are dependable, hardworking, trustworthy, and responsible. Similar to the Type One (the Reformer), the Type Six is excellent at identifying problems. However, what fuels this troubleshooting is their anxiety about anything and everything that could possibly go wrong. In response to their anxieties, they may go into overdrive trying to see things from every possible angle. One defining characteristic of a Type Six is their inner committee, which consists of different viewpoints and ideas. Sixes access their inner committees in all their decision-making.

Type Sixes are excellent planners who are detail-oriented and outstanding at managing people. Sixes are as equally great community leaders as they are friends. They are gifted at bringing together people from very different worlds and walks of life. Some challenges that Sixes may face stem from their struggles with anxiety. There are two types of Sixes: Phobic Sixes and Counterphobic Sixes. Phobic Sixes handle their anxiety by moving away from and avoiding the things that trigger their anxiety. Counterphobic Sixes handle their anxiety by springing into action against the fear, and they often appear like Type Eights (the Challengers), with their rule breaking and tough exterior.

Deep down, what Sixes are reacting to is feeling unsafe and needing to protect themselves from danger by attacking the very thing that is causing their fear and anxiety.

Like the Type Five (the Investigator), Sixes can be logical and cerebral. They are the best people to go to in emergencies because they have already thought of a plan A, plan B, and even a plan C. Among the values that a Type Six considers most important are trust and inner peace. Sixes need to trust themselves enough to make choices from a place free from fear. The Type Six's core fear is that they will be left without security or support in their time of need. They can often lean on either their internal committee or even an external one, asking friends and family for their opinions on thorny situations. Although Sixes value inner peace, getting access to it may be difficult for them because of a lack of self-trust.

An example of a Type Six in media is the character Dre Johnson from the TV show *Black-ish*. Although Dre is anxious about and suspicious of everything, he is an excellent team player and is exceptional at his job because of his ability to anticipate potential problems. In his family, Dre is the center. He's worked his whole life to create a better reality for his Black family living in a rich California suburb, and his anxiety and fear of it all being taken away from him motivate him to overanalyze and overthink all his life decisions and even the decisions of his children.

TYPE

7

THE ENNEAGRAM TYPE SEVEN IS SOMETIMES CALLED the Enthusiast or the Adventurer. A Type Seven's core desire is to be seen as a free person by themselves and others. They are motivated by a desire to live an exciting and fun life. Just as their nickname suggests, Sevens are seekers of adventure. They embrace spontaneity and often have diverse interests and hobbies. While they are typically extroverts, this may vary depending on their social position. Sevens are gifted at a lot of different things, which means that they often find themselves starting things they never finish. They can be scattered and distracted by the number of interests and projects they have on their plate, and they can overextend themselves because of their fear of missing out on new experiences.

Type Sevens lead with enthusiasm and joy in everything they do. They are skilled at

19

reframing negative experiences and emotions, but this can often lead to emotional or spiritual bypassing to avoid emotional distress within themselves and with other people. Type Sevens are also incredible conversationalists. They are talented storytellers with many anecdotes to share. However, people on the receiving end of conversations with a Seven may feel overpowered by their high energy and unheard or uninteresting because some Sevens struggle with being good listeners.

Like the Type Three (the Achiever), Type Sevens are the "yes" type, agreeing to try everything they can to keep life exciting and fulfilling. However, this desire to keep life interesting is often a mechanism to avoid painful experiences or a way of running from painful situations. It's difficult for Sevens to slow down long enough to feel the weight of all life's heaviness. After all, their core fear is that they will not be able to experience all that life has to offer and will be stuck in painful, uninspiring situations. Unlike the Type Four (the Individualist), Type Seven does not enjoy deep, dark, heavy emotions. They want to avoid these emotions for fear that they will be stuck in that mental state for long periods of time. However, Type Fours and Type Sevens are similar in their creative abilities and active imaginations.

An example of a Type Seven in media is the character Tamera Campbell from the TV Show *Sister, Sister*. Tamera often finds herself avoiding heavy responsibilities and embracing spontaneity in ways that her twin sister, Tia, does not. Because of this, Tamera ends up in sticky situations because her adventure seeking often prompts her to enlist her Type One twin sister to join in her exploits. Tamera's approach to life revolves around excitement and fun. Well into her college years, Tamera continues to embrace freedom and avoid pain. Her relationship with her boyfriend, Jordan, is an example of this. During times when Tamera is neglecting her responsibilities, Jordan calls her out, which leads to relational tension between the two.

TYPE

8

THE ENNEAGRAM TYPE EIGHT IS SOMETIMES CALLED the Challenger or the Protector. A Type Eight's core desire is to be seen as a strong person. They are motivated by a desire to ensure that harm does not come to them, that weakness does not stop them, and that they are in full control of their environment and life situations. Type Eights are not the type to back down from challenges. They meet conflict and threats head-on, with strength and power. They appear as unafraid and unintimidated by even the most prominent powers that be, and they willingly take them on. Like the Type Threes (the Achiever), Type Eights can make great leaders due to their ability to charm and persuade people. They are also similarly goal-oriented trailblazers, but Eights blaze trails to protect the weak and vulnerable; they are champions of justice and long to right wrongs. Eights can often be seen at the forefront of a battle, fighting for the "little guy." If they are not careful, Type

Eights' protectiveness can be perceived as bulldozing or controlling for those on the receiving end.

Eights try to avoid vulnerabilities at all costs. Their core fear is being seen as weak, so they are hypervigilant to potential harm that could come their way. Similar to the Counterphobic Six (the Loyalist), Eights cope with their anxiety and fear of feeling or being powerless by attacking that fear head-on. They have both a strong desire for independence and typically resist authorities who attempt to undermine their sense of autonomy. Like the Type Two (the Helper), Eights can struggle with saying no when they believe that their help or expertise is needed. They fear that if they do not help, no one else will be capable or strong enough to.

Eights are an incredibly resilient type. They can be knocked down seven times and get up eight. However, deep down, Type Eights long to feel safe and protected. Inside, Eights are not so tough. The time spent bottling up their feelings eventually catches up to them and they realize that they cannot take on the world by themselves. This is when they come to understand that vulnerability is strength and bulldozing the world only leads to burnout and resentment. Eights, in health, are described as tender and soft, but not in a way that makes them vulnerable to attack. They're tender with those who have proven to be safe for them. They willingly melt into the arms of the people they love and trust when the world seems heavier than they can bear. Eights desire to be held in both their strength *and* their vulnerabilities.

An example of a Type Eight in media is the character Philip Banks a.k.a. Uncle Phil from the TV show *The Fresh Prince of Bel-Air*. Uncle Phil exemplified the Type Eight personality structure in his approach to everything. After voluntarily housing his long-distance, Type Seven nephew, Will Smith, Uncle Phil puts a tight rein on Will to get him to assimilate to the life Uncle Phil has built for himself and his family. The tension between Type Seven and Type Eight personalities is evident here, as Uncle Phil and Will Smith are often at odds. However, in the moment when Will Smith is abandoned by his father for a second time, Uncle Phil steps in not only to defend and protect Will but also to embrace and comfort him.

TYPE

9

THE ENNEAGRAM TYPE NINE IS SOMETIMES CALLED the Peacemaker or the Mediator. A Type Nine's core desire is to be seen as a balanced person by themselves and others. They are motivated by a desire to ensure that they are creating a harmonious life, free of conflict and disagreements. Nines bring balance to the Enneagram. They move with grace, calmness, and a Zen-like outlook. They are typically slow-moving and mellow. Nines are easygoing and tolerant of all people, no matter what their differences. They tend to be liked and like anyone and everyone because of their sweet nature. Their serene energy gives them the tools they need to serve as an intermediary when their friends and family are in conflict.

Nines typically avoid attention. They do not want to "rock the boat," so they hide in the background to avoid the possibility of doing so. They may also struggle with decision-making because they fear their decision will cause disharmony and conflict, and Nines cannot handle being the cause of any feuds. Their core fear is that if they do not have peace or harmony within themselves and with others, they will experience loss and separation. This means that Type Nines often find themselves enmeshing with those around them. They become unaware of their own wants and needs because they have suppressed them so much to avoid problems in their relationships. Like the Type Two (the Helper), Nines are heavily relationship-focused individuals.

Nines value warmth and comfort. They often have certain items or people they cling to in moments of high stress or conflict in an attempt to ground themselves. They often resist change because it can mean possible loss of or separation from the way things are. Much like the Type Four (the Individualist), Nines have rich inner worlds. They are deep thinkers and seekers of meaning, and they are innately connected to the world around them.

In group settings, Nines often play the role of active listener, but they may not contribute much to the conversation, especially if dominant people are involved. During these moments, and in others when they feel a need to escape, the Type Nine will retreat into their mind. Their body may be present, but their thoughts and heart are elsewhere. Nines may be guilty of bottling up emotions. But if they are bottled up for too long, people in the Nine's life are likely to feel a wrath similar to that of the Type Eight (the Challenger)—explosions of frustration may occur as a result.

Like the Type Seven (the Enthusiast), Type Nines are great at seeing the silver lining in most situations. They have a positive outlook on life and want to protect themselves from getting too bogged down by difficult feelings, thoughts, and emotions.

An example of a Type Nine in media is the character Beth Pearson from the TV show *This Is Us*. Although always agreeable, Beth eventually must stand up for herself against her powerhouse of a husband, Randall. This only happens once she realizes that her entire life has been spent catering to his needs and not her own—a hard lesson for a Type Nine to have to learn.

CHAPTER TWO

The Nine Types in Love & Relationships

EACH ENNEAGRAM TYPE APPROACHES RELATIONships differently. While some types readily embrace love and romance, other types are more hesitant to engage in a relationship because of the possible threat to their autonomy. No matter the type, each one seeks love—and not just romantically. This chapter will mainly focus on romantic love, but the material can apply to platonic relationships as well. Use this chapter to reflect on how you can use your unique gifts to improve your relationships and as a mirror to show the ways in which you may be sabotaging your relationships.

It is also important to keep in mind type compatibility. Unlike other personality typing systems, the Enneagram makes it clear that all types are compatible—it just depends on their willingness to adapt their type for the sake of their relationships. Of course, some types may make better matches or complements for each other, but even those who are the best complements will ultimately face relational issues if they are not actively working on themselves. The healthiest relationships are formed when individuals are committed to becoming their best self for the good of the relationship.

Also in this chapter, we will be exploring a contemporary Enneagram concept called the Intelligence Centers. Understanding the Intelligence Centers will serve as a guide

to show how each type maneuvers relationships and love. These centers show the different ways in which we process and respond to life. The Intelligence Centers are broken down into a triad: the Gut Center, the Heart Center, and the Head Center, and you can see this presented in the image above. All types respond to and process life through either their body, their heart, or their mind.

Three types fall into each triad of the Intelligence Center: Types One, Eight, and Nine fall in the Gut Center. Types

Two, Three, and Four fall into the Heart Center. Types Five, Six, and Seven fall into the Head Center.

The first triad in the Intelligence Center is the Gut Center. Individuals guided by the Gut Center (Types One, Eight, and Nine) respond to and process life through their instincts and physical body. They are primarily concerned with justice and autonomy, and they may use anger as a way to achieve this. It is important to note that the three types that fall within this category all have a distinct relationship to anger. Type Ones repress their anger; Type Eights display their anger; and Nines deny their anger. Anger is their commonality, but the expression of the anger differs. In love and career, anger plays a key role in how they make decisions.

The second triad of the Intelligence Center is the Heart Center. Those who fall into the Heart Center (Types Two, Three, and Four) respond to and process life through their emotions and feelings. They are primarily concerned with image and attention, and they may use internal and external feelings of shame to achieve this. This may sound odd, but let me explain. Type Twos respond in order not to feel shame. They serve the people around them in hopes that service will alleviate the feeling of shame. Type Threes respond in order to resist shame. They achieve and collect accolades in hopes that the more they have attached to them, the less the feeling of shame will develop. Type Fours respond in order to avoid feeling deeper shame. Fours experience all emotions intensely, so they act to avoid more intense feelings of shame. All three types are feelings-based and are motivated to create a positive self-image. They are sensitive to emotional reactions and have the ability to connect and relate to others on different levels.

The third triad is the Head Center. Individuals who fall into the Head Center (Types Five, Six, and Seven) respond to and process life through their mind and logic. They are primarily concerned with strategy and safety, and they can use fears and anxiety as a way of achieving this. However, the manifestation of this is different for each of the three types. Type Fives' fears force them to isolate themselves. The Type Six's fears prompt them to constantly play worst-case scenarios in their minds. Type Sevens' fears force them to ignore and deny this fear by always keeping their mind and body busy.

Each of these Intelligence Centers play an important role and affect how the types respond to and process love, so we will touch on their influences on each of the nine types.

TYPE

1

THE ENNEAGRAM TYPE ONE IS DRIVEN BY PERFECTION-ism, even in relationships. They want to be the best version of themselves as a partner, and they strive to build the perfect relationship, often by being overly critical. Type Ones are the kind of partner who may benefit from regular check-ins to ensure that their partner feels supported by them. Ones will flourish if given space to share their grievances without judgment from their partner.

Other types may perceive Type Ones as too serious and overly focused on problems rather than on the good things happening in their relationships. They may feel as though Type Ones are placing too much pressure on themselves to perform and behave in a way they feel is most ideal; in reality, most people who are partnered with Type Ones care more about giving them space to show up as their authentic selves. Type Ones naturally have high expectations and standards, which are often (but not always) unattainable and can only really work in a perfect world. They have a vision for how they want their intimate relationships to be and will put in the work to make that vision a reality. They are committed to improving the relationship for the better, which means their partner will also improve as an individual. Ones are very good at prioritizing their partners and giving their best to the relationship.

Type Ones long to relax and enjoy life, but they may find it difficult to do so when they are hyperaware of all that is wrong in the world. In relationships, Ones are incredibly responsible and may feel that they are shouldering the burden of the relationship alone. They are incredibly supportive partners who desire to have a relationship shaped by integrity. Type Ones do best with someone who is dependable and reliable, someone who will show up for them when it counts. For Type Ones, a compatible partner is loyal and virtuous, aware of what it takes to make a relationship work and willing to put in the work to keep the relationship strong. Type Ones thrive when paired with someone with whom they can let their hair down. Finding a partner who carries their fair share of responsibilities will also go far for a Type One. Type Ones have perfectionist and communicative tendencies, meaning they are not the type to allow problems to linger and they won't sweep issues under the rug for the sake of peace.

Type Ones are located in the Gut Center. They often have a suppressed Heart Center, meaning they can struggle with connecting to their emotions. The Type One's communication style is direct and honest, and their experience of the world is more in tune with their internal sense of right and wrong. Ones may find it challenging to consider the feelings that come with responding to and processing emotions. The trick for the Type One is to mix this inner truth with grace; tact is the communication gift of the Type One when it comes to personal growth.

TYPE

2

TYPE TWOS ARE DRIVEN BY THE NEED TO PERFORM acts of service and helping their partners in relationships. They are great listeners who are deeply connected to their heart and make incredible romantic partners. Much of their behavior in relationships is motivated by an intrinsic need to be loved and appreciated by those they care about. Twos can be accommodating people who often give beyond what they have the capacity for; this can lead to burnout, pridefulness, and even resentment. They have a habit of putting others above themselves, and they are naturally fully invested in all their relationships. They often work hard to make sure their partner feels loved and appreciated—but they expect this to be reciprocated.

Other types may perceive the Type Two as overbearing because of their ability to anticipate needs. This skill may sometimes result in identifying needs that people do not want to be met—let alone met by the Two. This type can also be seen as manipulative. Because Type Twos are incredibly generous, they expect others to be the same in return. When their partner does not respond in kind, the Type Two may feel unappreciated, and they can resort to guilting their partner into behaving how they want them to.

Type Twos benefit from being paired with someone who reminds them that they are an equally important part of the relationship and that their needs matter just as much as their partner's. They need a partner who is intentional about reminding them of their worth outside of what the Type Two can do for them. Individuals who are selfish or are prone to taking advantage of people—unintentionally or otherwise—would not make ideal matches for a Two.

Like most other types, the Type Two needs to feel wanted and worthy. They desire to feel secure with their partner, whether through regular assurance or affirmation. They don't only need words; they need action. Type Twos need to feel and know they are irreplaceable.

Type Twos may struggle with connecting to their Gut Center and may have trouble communicating their needs. They may also find themselves disconnected from their own bodies because of their placement in Heart Center and how concerned they are about the well-being of those they love. It is imperative that Type Twos take time to care for themselves and meet their own needs; regular check-ins are key for this type's growth.

TYPE

3

TYPE THREES ARE DRIVEN BY COMMITMENT AND dedication in relationships. Like most of us, they value loyalty and integrity above all. It is imperative for the Type Three to know what their partner thinks of them on a regular basis. Type Threes desire a relationship filled with success and satisfaction. They want to know that their partner is proud of them *and* proud to be with them.

Other types may find the Type Three to be honest, direct, and straightforward. Threes are very clear about what they desire in a relationship and have no problems communicating this to a future partner. On the flip side, others may also find this type to be self-centered and preoccupied with how they appear to others.

Type Threes long to be fully known and seen beyond their accomplishments. They need to know that their partner values them outside of what they do and the success they have achieved. Threes desperately want to take off their mask and connect deeply to their partner in an intimate way. Their ideal partner provides a place for the Three to let their guard down and be their true self, not the self that they have curated for attention and affection. They seek to be loved for who they truly are. Knowing that someone sees past their mask is a balm for the Type Three's soul.

Threes benefit from a partner who understands their need to be productive. An ideal partner can provide them with the space and time to work toward their goals but also reminds them that rest is just as important as work. Type Threes benefit from being in relationships with people who are able to slow down and connect with their emotions, since this is something that Threes tend to struggle with. A partner like this provides much-needed balance.

Type Threes are ruled by the Heart Center so they may struggle to connect to their body. Like the Type Two, Type Threes are not especially in tune with their own needs. They may know how to meet the expectations of their partners but are often unsure of what support or help they themselves need. Additionally, Threes can often be workaholics who are unaware of their limits and can spread themselves too thin. If they are not careful, productivity and success may take precedence over their relationships. Type Threes should be mindful about the amount of time they spend pursuing their goals as opposed to the time they spend investing in their relationships.

TYPE

IN RELATIONSHIPS, TYPE FOURS ARE DRIVEN BY THE desire to have an extraordinary love. They are the true romantics of the Enneagram. They desire relationships that are special and unique. They are empathetic people whose access to deep emotions serve them well, especially once they go through the inevitable ups and downs of relationships. Fours are particularly sensitive to the needs of their partner, and they can sense even the slightest change in their tone or energy. The Type Four values depth in all their relationships. They want to know all that there is to know about their beloved, which can sometimes feel intrusive if the relationship is new.

Other types may find the Type Four to be overly dramatic at times. Fours can also be perceived as being too vulnerable by some. Some may find a Type Four's presence a safe space where they can show up authentically because of how open and vulnerable the Four is willing to be. Fours often tend to be "open books" who enjoy sharing things that would take the other eight Enneagram types significant time to reveal. But because they value depth and yearn to be deeply known, they are more willing to disclose personal thoughts, ideas, and feelings to new people.

Although they long to feel things intensely, Fours should be wary about getting trapped in them. It serves a Four well to learn how to balance the emotions and the mundane tasks of everyday life. Fours flourish when they find a partner who can respond to them in both their lightness and their heaviness, in both their sunshine and their darkness. They should not get stuck in emotional darkness alone. To avoid this, Type Fours benefit from being with someone who is emotionally balanced. Fours need to put in the work themselves, so partnering with someone who encourages them to find this balance is imperative to their personal growth and emotional health. A partner who is emotionally aware and sensitive to their needs is ideal for a Type Four. They also thrive when being showered with compliments and words of affirmation.

Type Fours are individualists, so finding a partner who respects their need for freedom and expression is vital to their well-being. Because of this, Fours may find themselves drawn to expressive and direct people, sensitive to changes in their partner. Finding someone who is a clear communicator and is unafraid to talk about how they feel in a thoughtful and intentional way goes far for a Four.

Type Fours may struggle with connecting to their Head Center because of how deeply connected they are to their Heart Center. Fours can become so tangled up in their emotional experience that they may forget that reality exists. Logic and reason are not always compatible with feeling and emotion, so the Type Four often chooses feelings over logic because that is their natural baseline. Equanimity may rescue the Type Four from experiencing the heavy weight of their emotions. Type Fours' ability to live deeply connected to themselves in a spiritual way, without losing sight of the everyday tasks that need to be completed, helps them find balance within themselves and their relationships.

TYPE

5

TYPE FIVES FAVOR INDEPENDENCE AND UNDERSTAND-ing in relationships. They have a strong desire to avoid relationships that demand too much of their resources—like time, energy, and space. They are slow-moving and in no rush to enter into a partnership because they recognize how demanding committed relationships can be. They want to be competent and capable in their relationships, so they are constantly learning and growing. Fives may find relationships intimidating. They may feel inadequate and ill-equipped to take on the challenges of romantic intimacy. To curb this fear, Fives may read books and find other resources on relationships and love to ensure that they are prepared to handle whatever is thrown at them once they decide to engage in a romantic partnership.

Other types may see Type Fives as withdrawn, detached, and even cold. In reality, the Five is simply taking in experiences through intense observation. Inside, Type Fives are naturally loyal, intelligent, and creative people. They make excellent life partners once they get out of their heads and move into their hearts. Much like the Type Four, Type Fives are afraid of being seen as too much. Unlike the

Four, who proudly shines loudly and brightly, Fives can be seen as shrinking themselves to avoid appearing like this. A Five's ideal partner is someone who encourages them to ask for more. They thrive with someone who reminds them of the abundance life has to offer, an optimistic and good-natured partner who sees the glass as half full. Fives do not enjoy being smothered with affection or clinginess, and they often give their partner a lot of space. Because of this, Type Fives thrive with a partner who does well on their own. Independence is attractive to this type. Someone willing to listen and sit under the wisdom of the Type Five also makes for a good partner. Type Fives enjoy sharing the things they've learned with those they love, so it is important for the Five to pair with someone who enthusiastically listens to their latest obsession. It may take a while for a Type Five to open up, so whomever they partner with must be comfortable with giving them space and time to share when they feel ready. Fives do not like feeling rushed into revealing what's in their hearts.

Type Fives may struggle with connecting to their Heart Center because they are caught up in the safety of their own mind. Feelings and emotions are difficult to hold alongside logic, so the Type Five often chooses logic over feelings and emotions. They are not particularly emotionally expressive people, but they tend to try to make sense of their emotions by thinking about them rather than feeling them. However, Fives are deep feelers whose default is not to dive headfirst into their emotions the way a Type Four might. The Type Five is more concerned about practical things they can make sense of.

TYPE

6

TYPE SIXES ARE DRIVEN BY SAFETY AND LOYALTY IN relationships. They value commitment both toward their partner and from their partner. They rarely end relationships over small quarrels or disagreements. Sixes desire to always be there for the people they love and fight hard for their relationships. They are champions of their partner and defend them, no matter the situation. In general, Sixes are not risk-takers if the situation is not dire. They enjoy solving problems for their loved ones and do so by assessing situations from every angle.

Other types may experience the Type Six as responsible and hardworking. But they may also feel that the Six is controlling and leery of their partner's decision-making abilities. Sixes want to feel prepared for anything; if they have a partner who leans more spontaneous, this preparation may seem stifling. Because the Type Six is a natural skeptic who values security so highly in relationships, others may view the Six as someone with trust issues or insecurities.

The Type Six's main desires in a relationship are commitment and consistency. They trust themselves enough to trust those they decide to spend their time with. Honesty and transparency are huge factors for a Type Six in love because clear communication is one of the ways they build trust. Feeling trust and security in their relationships soothes any worries about being blindsided by hidden agendas and behaviors.

A Type Six benefits from finding a partner who is incredibly supportive of them and who values loyalty and commitment just as much they do. They cherish a partner who can take them out of their comfort zone in a gentle way. They need a partner who is comfortable with verbally expressing commitment and also showing the Type Six, through action, that they are all-in on the relationship. Sixes can struggle with deciding if they can trust their partner, so it is imperative for them to be with someone who does not have sneaky or manipulative tendencies.

Sixes may struggle with connecting to the Gut Center. They are based in the Head Center and have an inner committee they can go to for advice and direction. This inner committee offers different perspectives and solutions to problems that may arise within their relationship. Because their inner committee is such an integral part of their makeup, the Type Six may struggle with trusting themselves and others. They may rely on logic so much that they struggle to trust their intuition and listen to how their body feels. This may explain why the Type Six may choose to stay in a toxic relationship—their sense of loyalty and commitment may take precedence over obvious signals that it is time to end the relationship.

TYPE

7

TYPE SEVENS ARE DRIVEN BY THE DESIRE TO FEEL FREE and spontaneous in relationships. They lead their lives with high energy and an eagerness to experience all that life has to offer. Sevens often have a childlike aura that makes them charismatic and charming people. They may also be thrilled at the prospect of new love because of their inherent curiosity and adventure seeking. They take great delight in exploring everything about their partner.

Other types may experience the Type Seven as romantic and passionate, since they are so full of curiosity and eagerness for new ventures. Type Sevens view love as something to be excited about, and they may dream of all the ways they can bring their partner along on their adventures and experience their passions together.

Sevens thrive if they feel that their commitment to their partner is not a trap or a death sentence for their freedom. They want to experience love as a liberating and freeing thing rather than a stifling and limiting relationship. Because of their love of adventure, Type Sevens may struggle with commitment. They are often found jumping from experience to experience to keep the thrill alive. Even when they know that their partner is right for them, they find it difficult to commit because that can make them feel tied down. They don't want to feel bored in their relationships, so it's important for the Seven to pair with someone who is a healthy mix of both secure *and* open-minded.

Matching a Type Seven in energy and passion is helpful, but finding someone who can restore balance to their lives is also important. This is why Type Sevens may feel drawn to more serious types, like Type Ones or Type Eights. They enjoy spending time with individuals who are reliable and stable. Sevens also need a partner who can handle them when they are in growth and begin acknowledging and feeling difficult emotions. A partner who judges them or expects them to stay positive and light when life is difficult will not have long-term success with a Type Seven. Eventually, the mask of positivity comes down, and the Type Seven needs to know they can show their darker side without that changing the way their partner views them.

Type Sevens may struggle with connecting to their Heart Center. They may want to avoid feelings of pain and distress, so they'll often downplay distressing situations with positivity and good vibes or even by ignoring them altogether. A Type Seven's partner may find it hard to invite the Seven into heavy and difficult feelings that can potentially make them feel trapped. It's helpful if the Type Seven is paired with someone who has good access to their Heart Center and who is incredibly patient and understanding of the Type Seven's core desires and fears.

TYPE

8

TYPE EIGHTS ARE DRIVEN BY A DESIRE TO FEEL PRO-tected and safe in relationships. Eights are dependable and reliable partners who do whatever is needed to make sure their partner is safe. They are protective of their loved ones and happily come to their defense if an occasion demands it. Eights value their autonomy and independence and, much like Type Sevens, do not want to feel as though their partner is controlling them.

Some types may find Eights to be aggres-sive and controlling, but when the Type Eight feels safe with someone, they let their guard down, becoming soft and tender with the ones they love. People in love with a Type Eight often get to experience a side of them that they do not readily show. Eights can often be seen as great providers and pro-tectors by their partners. Type Eights know how to create a safe and secure environment for their loved ones when they are healthy. When they are not healthy, Type Eights can be perceived as demanding, bossy, headstrong, and intense. Health, for the Type Eight, can be described as a willingness to let their guard down and let people in.

Type Eights long to feel safe in their partnership. They want to know they are connected to someone who is strong and won't be intimidated by them. They also want to feel that their partner is someone they can let their guard down with. They want to know that their partner holds space for their soft and tender spots and doesn't exploit their vulnerability.

Type Eights flourish with a partner they believe is their equal in most ways. Type Eights benefit from a partner who is able to slowly draw their emotions out of them. It is important for the Type Eight to pair with someone who can stand up for themselves and express their own needs. An Eight often avoids relationships with people who are pushy and demanding. Like Type Fives, Eights do not enjoy being in a relationship with people who try to control them or demand specific behaviors from them in order to be happy.

The Type Eight often struggles with connecting to their Heart Center because of how much they want to avoid vulnerability and feelings of weakness in all areas of their life, with love being no exception. Love is often the riskiest thing we can experience in life, so the Type Eight often approaches it with a tight fist, testing their partner's ability to handle them. Eights may also find that they struggle with asking for help in relationships because of their desire to avoid situations that make them vulnerable. They want to feel in charge and in control of their emotions and feelings. Because of these fears, they often feel more easily able to express emotions—such as anger rather than sadness or fear—in front of others.

TYPE

9

THE TYPE NINE IS DRIVEN BY A DESIRE TO LIVE AT PEACE with themselves and others in relationships. They are naturally patient and accommodating, often finding themselves going along with whatever their partner wants in order to avoid conflict and maintain a sense of peace within the relationship. Nines often get comfortable in their relationships and avoid change. Type Nines are incredibly supportive partners who practice nonjudgment and kindness.

When the Type Nine is unhealthy and has gone too long without expressing their needs and desires, others can experience them as passive-aggressive. Others may experience the Type Nine as a calming presence because they naturally know how to ease tension in any room. It's imperative for the Type Nine to get in touch with their voice.

Because Type Nines are in the Gut Center, they have a keen relationship to their physical bodies and tangible environments. Type Nines' relationship to their body shows up in the ways in which they create comfort for themselves in their home, their car, their workplace, etc. While Type Nines work to ensure they are at peace in their body, they are unsure about what they truly want in their own hearts. This means they have trouble acting on their wants when the wants of another contradict their own. It often leads them to concede or acquiesce to avoid conflict. In a relational conflict, Nines don't want to think too hard about the issues in the relationship because, if they acknowledge those issues, it often disrupts their inner peace. This avoidance of conflict can be difficult for someone partnered with the Type Nine to grapple with, especially if they are an Enneagram type that is comfortable with conflict, like the Type Eight and Type One.

Nines simply want to experience tranquility in their life, both internally and externally. They want to experience life as peaceful and balanced while having their needs and desires met by their partner. While supporting their partner and making them a priority, Nines also want their partner to support them and make them a priority. Mutuality is important in all relationships for all types but Nines are especially sensitive to this. They want their relationship connections to be spiritual not surface-level.

It is important for the Type Nine to pair with someone who is not going to take advantage of their accommodating nature. Instead, they should look to forge a relationship with someone who encourages the Nine to advocate for their needs. A partner who checks in with the Type Nine regularly to make sure that they feel they're getting what they need from the relationship is a great fit for them. Nines are incredibly sensitive to their partners, so it's important that they couple up with someone who shares this trait. A Type Nine may find themselves drawn to Type Twos and Type Fours because of how deeply connected both of these types are to their hearts. Because Type Nines are not always overly ambitious, it might be helpful for the Nine to pair with someone who is ambitious to balance out the energies. Type Threes and Type Nines are a common pairing because of this.

Type Nines often struggle with accessing their Head Center. They may find it difficult to express their thoughts and share their feelings with their partner. They know what they feel and think, and they often experience those feelings in their body, yet they may have trouble finding a way to communicate what they are experiencing. They may also mesh with the feelings and thoughts of others while ignoring their own wants and needs. Growth for the Type Nine within a relationship involves rediscovering their voice and confidently expressing their thoughts and feelings with their loved ones.

CHAPTER THREE

The Nine Types
in Career

THE CAREER LIFE OF EACH TYPE DIFFERS DEPEND-
ing on the level of awareness that each individual
holds. Aware individuals are more likely to choose
jobs that align with their unique gifts. Unaware individuals
may choose jobs that align with society's expectations of
them, even if the expectation is out of alignment with who
they are and what they want from life. This chapter is meant
to invoke self-reflection, since work can take up a large and
important part of our lives.

TYPE

1

THE TYPE ONE IS THE NATURAL BOSS OF THE WORK-
place. They are ethical, practical, action-oriented individuals. Their organizational skills and coordinating abilities
prepare them well for many different careers. They find it
very important to approach everything they do through a
lens of perfection and excellence. Type Ones are also very
loyal. Typically, once they have found an organization or
team that they align with, they commit themselves to doing
their best work in that space. They're excellent
problem solvers and can spot mistakes others might miss.

However, Type Ones may face some pitfalls in the workplace, such as the "If you
want something done right, you need to do
it yourself" mentality. This outlook means
they are often shouldering the burden of
responsibility alone, often micromanaging
their team. Similar to how they are in relationships, Type Ones may hold themselves
and others to extremely high standards.
Tensions may flare when a Type One's

ideal rubs up against another type's good-enough outlook at work. Type Ones may come across as highly critical to the individuals they supervise.

The best career options for Type Ones are those where they can embrace fun and spontaneity alongside responsibility and excellence. The key for the Type One is to experience work as fulfilling and meaningful. Type Ones also work best in environments where the rules are clear and the standards are high. Organizations where chaos and disorder are prevalent create stress and anxiety for this type. Careers focused on fairness, justice, and equality would be ideal for the Type One because these are their core values.

TYPE

2

TYPE TWOS ARE NATURAL RELATIONSHIP BUILDERS in the workplace. They find fulfillment in knowing that their work is contributing to the greater good. Type Twos are gifted at creating a warm and safe environment for their coworkers, employers, and employees. As the colleague who bakes cookies for the office, hosts office events, and organizes other gatherings that boost morale, they are deeply connected to their coworkers and want to know them beyond the surface level. Type Twos strive to have their work enrich the lives of the people on their team. Motivated by the desire to be admired and appreciated by these people, Twos long to be thought well of and enjoy doing work that gives them room to flex their empathetic skills. They enjoy being liked and known for their irreplaceable characteristics around the workplace. A pitfall for Type Twos is that they often try to be everything to everyone. They can get caught up in being so helpful that they neglect their own responsibilities. Their focus on relationships may also interfere with their productivity and get in the way of completing the job if they are not careful. Type Twos may also struggle with not being liked by others. They may encounter a coworker, employer, or employee who does not particularly care for their company, and this can greatly affect the Type Two because of how important relationships are to them.

The best career options for Type Twos are careers that value relationship building and are customer-/client-facing. Type Twos are often drawn to nonprofit work, careers working with kids or other vulnerable populations like animals or the elderly, and therapy or counseling work. Type Twos can leverage their patient, kind, and compassionate personality traits in careers that give them room to be themselves. However, the Type Two should be careful to choose a career that will not take advantage of their willingness to go above and beyond for the greater good. Type Twos benefit from learning how to establish and enforce their boundaries.

TYPE

3

TYPE THREES ARE NATURAL HARD WORKERS, MAKING them a valuable asset in any workplace. They are inspiring role models who many people look up to. They have clear goals and are driven to accomplish these goals. Type Threes are wonderful at meeting and exceeding the expectations of their employers. They value straightforward and clear communication so that they fully understand what is needed from them in order to do their job. Like most people, they work best with specific instructions because of their desire to achieve exactly what is expected of them. They are confident, charismatic people who like to complete a job in the most efficient way possible. Threes may be afraid of feeling like they are a failure, so they tend to do almost anything to alleviate those feelings. Words of affirmation and positive reinforcement go far. While they may appear self-assured, sometimes this can mask insecurities or a sense of inadequacy.

For the Type Three, a pitfall of all their hard work and goal orientation is a tendency toward workaholism; burnout; and emotional, physical, and mental exhaustion. They may become overly competitive and impatient in the face of distractions and interruptions when they are in the zone. Type Threes do not want to say no, and this can mean taking on heavy workloads—even when they realistically cannot handle them. The Type Three may also struggle with being too concerned with what other people think of them, causing them to lose touch with how they feel about themselves. Threes should find careers where they can take regular breaks. Careers that reward overworking will prove unsustainable for the Type Three if they do not have boundaries in place to avoid this.

Because the Type Three is known as the Performer, the best career options for them should involve anything that leaves them feeling a sense of accomplishment and admiration. They make excellent entrepreneurs and can be internally driven enough to handle the pressures of working for themselves. They believe deeply in their ability to succeed. Type Threes also excel in careers where they are the leader. At their best, they are amazing at managing people and working efficiently because they easily inspire people. Type Threes would also make effective motivational speakers because of their charisma and encouraging personalities.

TYPE

THE ENNEAGRAM TYPE FOUR IS THE NATURAL CREATIVE in the workplace who offers many gifts. They are the ones who think outside the box, creating innovative ideas and processes. They are inspiring individuals whose sense of purpose and self-awareness enables them to see the beauty in all things. They also have the ability to find meaning in anything.

A pitfall for the Type Four is that their melancholy may get in the way of completing a job. Being able to hold difficult feelings can be a hindrance for the Type Four if they are unable to adequately process those feelings without becoming overwhelmed by them.

The best career options for the Type Four are careers that allow them to express themselves fully. Fours benefit from working for organizations whose mission and values align with their own. For example, if a Type Four values sustainability and reducing environmental waste, it would be difficult for them to work for an organization that does not also hold this value. Many Type Fours choose creative careers where they are their own boss. If they decide to work for an organization where creativity is limited, Type Fours often have an actively creative hobby that they engage in regularly to balance out the structured nature of their career.

TYPE

5

THE ENNEAGRAM TYPE FIVE IS A NATURAL EXPERT IN the workplace. They are the curious, analytical, intelligent, independent sages of the office. Their expertise enriches any workplace they enter. Most Type Fives tend to be introverts, so they will likely spend their entire workday with their head down and working hard rather than socializing like the Type Two or the Type Seven. Type Fives are motivated by the need to be competent and capable, and there is no place where this is more valued than in the workplace. A Five will do their best to learn whatever they need to in order to be a valuable asset to the company.

Pitfalls for the Type Five are that they can be withdrawn, closed off, and very independent. Coworkers may not know much about the Type Five's life outside the office. They may be private people who like to keep their work life separate from their personal life. They are not likely to attend after-work functions with their coworkers if their working relationships have not graduated from colleague to friend. Just as they are in relationships, Fives are particular about how they spend their time and energy.

The best career options for the Type Five are those where learning never ends. A Type Five's desire for knowledge must be met for them to find any sense of fulfillment at work. Fives benefit from careers that are not heavily dependent on teamwork because of their introversion and need for independence. However, Type Fives would greatly benefit from careers that force them out of their comfort zone. The sweet spot for the Type Five would be a career that is service-oriented but that also requires niche expertise in a certain field. For example, they may feel comfortably stretched in customer-facing software engineer roles and reasonably challenged in nurse practitioner roles that require niche expertise but are deeply service oriented. A career like this will provide growth opportunities and the ability to flex their natural skills and talents.

TYPE

6

THE ENNEAGRAM TYPE SIX IS THE NATURAL PROBLEM solver in the workplace, identifying and resolving potential issues before they escalate. They can see things from every angle and often consult their infamous inner committee about issues they encounter. Having a Type Six on your team improves the quality of the plans or projects you're developing. They value connection and relationships in the workplace so they may be involved in both planning and coordinating work-place events. Their natural community-building skills come in handy often.

The Type Six encounters some pitfalls when they offer opinions and thoughts on potential problems in a blunt way, causing coworkers to view their input as nega-tive. It's important for the Six to offer advice using a "feedback sandwich": Start with positive reinforcement by letting their team know what is good and right about the plan or project. Follow this by sharing the potential issues and problems, and then finish off with a reminder of the positive aspects. This technique makes it easier for people receiving the feedback to know that the intentions behind it are good.

The best career options for the Sixes are those that involve a high level of responsibility, commitment, care, and compassion. The Type Six thrives when they get to work on teams, so any career that allows them to be part of something bigger than themselves will be a good fit. Careers that allow only independent work should be avoided. Sixes should avoid careers that cause them anxiety, like unstable, unreliable careers that require frequent change. If they are an employee, it's important for their employer to be equally as hardworking and collaborative as they are.

TYPE

THE ENNEAGRAM TYPE SEVEN IS THE CREATIVE IDEA generator in the workplace. They can think of unique ways to solve problems, often leaning on their Type Six wing, if they have one, to find a solution. Sevens bring their high energy and desire for newness to the workplace to serve as innovators and thought leaders in whatever space they inhabit. They bring joy and fun to every environment. They are quick learners and very adaptable to new situations and environments. They tend to be invested in the people at their workplace, so you'll rarely find them in careers that don't involve some type of interaction with others.

While Type Sevens are creative idea generators, they often can lack follow-through. They may take on numerous projects simultaneously but may not finish them if they get bored or lose interest. Their spontaneity makes them adaptable, but it also means that they can jump from one project to another. Type Sevens would benefit from working in teams with people—like Type Ones, Threes, Sixes, and Eights—who are skillful at executing their ideas alongside them.

The best career options for the Type Seven are those that are fast-paced and allow them to draw on their charisma, energy, and spontaneity. They thrive in careers that have some sort of flexibility and adventure involved. Careers that force the Type Seven to pay attention to details are difficult because they are more big-picture thinkers than they are detail-oriented. They can make great entrepreneurs when they partner with someone who can help with the administrative side of the business. Type Sevens enjoy interacting with people so they should avoid careers that are not client-/customer-facing. They cannot handle being bored, so they will likely change their careers over their lifetime. Type Sevens find fulfillment in careers where their ideas and optimism are appreciated. The worst careers for a Seven are those that force them to sit in one place for hours alone behind a desk. They are likely to avoid careers that are heavy and involve a lot of pain or hurt such as counseling people through deep, complex trauma.

TYPE

8

THE ENNEAGRAM TYPE EIGHT IS THE NATURAL LEADER in the workplace. Their willpower is incomparable. They are charming and great at convincing people to join their cause—whatever it may be. Eights are champions of justice and fairness and make great advocates for the underdog. They lead with their powerful demeanor and decisive nature. They know who they are, what they want, and how to get it. They are comfortable with taking on a more dominant role in the workplace because of their confidence in themselves and their abilities.

Some pitfalls for the Type Eight are that they can be confrontational and harsh, which can be difficult for people who are sensitive to criticism. As a boss, Eights may often appear to be both protective and overbearing. They have access to all their emotions but naturally express anger most easily, which can be jarring in moments of high stress.

The best career options for the Type Eight are ones that allow them to experience autonomy and independence. They value careers where they feel respected by their peers. The Type Eight prefers to work with individuals who understand that their intentions are good and pure. Eights also make great entrepreneurs because of their ability to pave their own paths without interference of others. They may thrive in careers that allow them to promote justice, as well as in competitive careers. Eights may feel drawn to career paths that are highly respected in society. Type Eights are unlikely to thrive in careers where they feel like they need to cater to the feelings of others.

TYPE

THE ENNEAGRAM TYPE NINE IS THE CONNECTOR IN the workplace. They are gifted at bringing people together and helping them all get along. They often serve as the mediator for their coworkers, standing in the breach to ensure that harmony reigns in their workplace relationships. Nines are able to serve as this middle person because of their ability to see things objectively. They see the world from many perspectives and understand that one way is not better than the other. Their calming energy makes it easy for people to listen to them. Type Nines tend to bring a much-welcome serene energy to the workplace. Although they are not usually the assertive type (and generally take on supportive roles), they do make great leaders but are not often found in these positions.

A pitfall for the Type Nine in the workplace is a tendency to be overly accommodating. They may find themselves enmeshed in other people's desires for them. They may not be fully aware of what it is *they* want from their own career experience. Type Nines tend to find it easy to connect with other people, but this natural ability also means that the Type Nine will be influenced by a lot of people's opinions and thoughts on what they should do with their career. The challenge for the Type Nine is to ensure that they take control of their career and that they are not being influenced to move in directions that are not in alignment with who they are and what they truly want out of life.

The best career options for the Type Nine are those that give them access to nature and spirituality. They want to feel connected to the earth but also deeply connected to people. They are highly motivated to find careers that give their inner world a sense of relief and rest. Type Nines can truly make any career a spiritual practice, so whatever they decide to do often goes in this direction. Type Nines benefit from careers that have some sort of service component to them. Careers that allow the Type Nine to be in sync with the world and others is a surefire win for them. Type Nines may benefit from looking into careers that involve projects and clients that speak to them internally such as counseling, yoga/meditation instructor, or social work.

CONCLUSION

THE ENNEAGRAM IS A MULTIFACETED SYSTEM THAT can reveal fascinating truths about your personality. Understanding the different ways in which your Enneagram type affects your everyday life, your relationships, and even your career is invaluable to both your personal growth and for the health of your community. I hope this book gives you insight into some of the traits and motivations that influence you.

Speaking of community, I want to encourage you to engage with the Enneagram in a community setting. In the modern world, we are used to doing things as individuals. I believe that our collective liberation and growth come from being able to lean on the wisdom and gifts of the other types. Engaging the Enneagram in community is not only a gift to you but a gift to the people you are loving, living, and working with.

One of the ways you can do this is by finding a few friends you trust with your story to discuss the Enneagram. Consider enrolling in an introductory Enneagram course led by diverse and inclusive groups. Jessica D. Dickson, an Enneagram and Anti-racism coach and teacher, often states that we cannot divorce our Enneagram work from Anti-racism work.

There are seemingly endless resources you can use to expand your knowledge of the Enneagram. My hope is that this book will guide you on your Enneagram journey. But don't stop here. Keep exploring. May your path be full of joy and illuminating discovery.

RESOURCES

BOOKS

Agorom, Chichi, *The Enneagram for Black Liberation*, Broadleaf
Books (March 29, 2022)

Chestnut, Beatrice, *The Complete Enneagram*, She Writes Press
(July 31, 2013)

Egerton, Deborah, *Know Justice, Know Peace*, Hay House LLC
(September 6, 2022)

Riso, Don Richard and Russ Hudson. *The Wisdom of the Enneagram*,
Bantam (June 15, 1999)

YOUTUBE CHANNELS

Abbey Howe, https://www.youtube.com/@AbbeyHowe

Frank James, https://www.youtube.com/@FrankJames

You've Got a Type, https://www.youtube.com/@YouveGotaType

ANTI-RACISM AND ENNEAGRAM COACHES
AND COMPANIES

Danielle Fanfair / Confusion to Clarity,
https://www.confusiontoclarity.life/

Deborah Egerton / Trinity Transition Consultants,
https://www.trinitytransition.com/

Jessica D. Dickson / The Antiracist Enneagram,
https://jessicaddickson.com/

Milton Stewart / Kaizen Careers, Coaching and Consulting,
https://kaizencareers.com/services

The Narrative Enneagram, https://www.narrativeenneagram.org/

INSTAGRAM PAGES TO FOLLOW

Ashlee, @nineshapes

Beth McCord, @yourenneagramcoach

Camille and Kim, @enneagramfortheculture

Danielle Fanfair, @danielle_fanfair

Funlola, @enneagrameverything

Jamila, @typesinblackink

Jessica D Dickson, @jessicaddickson and @jessicaddicksoncoaching

Milton Stewart, @doitforthegrampodcast

Steph Barron, @ninetypesco

NOTES

NOTES

ABOUT THE AUTHOR

DAYO AJANAKU, the visionary behind The Black Enneagram, is a dynamic force in the Enneagram space. Raised in Houston, Texas, Dayo's journey into the world of the Enneagram began as a personal quest for growth and evolved into a desire to explore the intersections of the Enneagram, Black art and media, and faith. In 2020, she founded The Black Enneagram, a digital sanctuary with the goals of increasing self-awareness and promoting self-actualization and community health, specifically in the Black community. Through engaging content and thought-provoking discussions, Dayo has cultivated a vibrant online community with an unwavering commitment to amplify marginalized voices within the Enneagram community. Dayo is a graduate of Agnes Scott College and the University of California Berkeley School of Law and is currently a practicing attorney in California. She is also the writer of RP's *Everyday Enneagram*, a mini deck and book.